Life-Changing Letters

Brianna Pritchard

A special thanks to my love, Shelby, and all who've ever lent me a listening ear, a shoulder to cry on, or a compassionate heart.

My Letter

Whether it's because of my birthday, Christmas, 11:11, or a shooting star, any opportunity for me to make a wish is met with a sigh. Not a here-we-go-again sigh, but one resulting from the realization that my wish will not be granted—will *never* be granted. At least, that's how it seems right now. You'd think my wish involves some sort of miracle, a longing so farfetched and unrealistic that would force me to recognize its impossibility. But no. My wish, though intangible, is completely within reach, just not within *my* reach. What I wish for, more than anything, is acceptance.

*   *   *

During my junior year of college, I developed a crush like many I've had before. The only difference with this one was my decision to acknowledge it rather than push it aside and pretend it wasn't there. My crush was on a female friend with whom I had been spending a lot of time. I didn't just enjoy hanging out with her; I felt something inside, something I couldn't ignore. Rather than keep the secret to myself, I decided to express my feelings to Nikki through writing. A few nights later, though extremely nervous to do so, I handed her a letter. As she read its content, my embarrassment radiated from head to toe, and I started to second-guess my decision. When Nikki finished reading, she looked up at me. I expected to see anger or disgust in her expression, but what I saw instead was compassion and understanding. We talked for a while about my feelings, and in a very nonjudgmental manner, she admitted I might be gay, bisexual, or at least curious.

The next day, I confided in my best friend Paul about this situation, and he was nothing but supportive. He understood that my feelings must have been confusing and offered his best advice. Little by little, I started spilling my guts to other friends I could trust, and I received no distaste whatsoever. In fact, I received encouragement. I was told to explore my feelings because they wouldn't simply go away.

I knew one lesbian on campus, and I reached out to her. After a long heart-to-heart, Jen sent me on my way with Season One of *The L Word* (a lesbian television series), some pamphlets from the GLBTQ center on campus, and the afterthoughts of a much needed conversation. Walking back to my dorm, I somehow knew my life would never be the same.

I needed to sort through my feelings, but I didn't know how or with whom. So, after a few weeks, I decided to try online dating. I wasn't openly gay/bi, and since I didn't "look" gay either, I thought there was no other way to find a girl. I made a profile on the web and listed myself as bisexual. Interestingly enough, I met a nice guy I went to dinner with after some time, but there was no spark. I then started talking to a girl named Kayla, but after getting together a few times, she suggested we remain friends. *This isn't working,* I kept thinking to myself. *I just want to know who I am, but I can't do that until I've at least kissed a girl.*

*   *   *

A week later, I started exchanging messages with another girl, and after three successful dates, she came to Kutztown

University to meet my friends and spend the night. That was the first time I had ever introduced my friends to a girl who wasn't just a friend, and the first time they had seen me interact with one. It couldn't have gone more smoothly. Erin fit right in, and we all had a great time. Paul, who noticed my obnoxious radiance, pulled her aside and thanked her for being the reason I had such a huge smile on my face. Toward the end of our night, I led Erin onto the roof to gaze at the stars, where I proceeded to read a poem I wrote about her. We shared a kiss after the last line, and later that night slept with our arms around each other. I knew—I just knew!—that was how it was supposed to feel. It wasn't the same as kissing Mark, Korey, Chris, or Matt, just to name the guys I had kissed up to that point. Kissing and cuddling with Erin didn't just feel normal. It felt right. It felt perfect.

Erin went home in the morning, and a few hours later sent me a message suggesting we just be friends. She could tell I wanted a relationship and didn't want the same. I was crushed. I finally found someone who lit a flicker of light inside of me, and it was so quickly extinguished. I ran to Paul's apartment crying, and all my friends were there to comfort me. Although my experience with Erin ended in heartbreak, dating her for that short period confirmed that I do, in fact, like women.

After a week of ignoring Erin, I gradually started talking to her again as a friend. She encouraged me to tell my parents about my interest in girls. I didn't see the point considering I had no girlfriend, but she explained I didn't need to have a girlfriend to tell them—having one was just an accessory. I knew my parents would be hurt by the news, so I was hesitant. Ultimately, though, I decided it was the right thing to do. After carefully crafting a heartfelt letter, one that I revised over and over and had several of my friends cry while reading, I decided to send it. At the time, I didn't know mailing that letter would be the worst decision I could have ever made. . . .

Dear Mom and Dad,

    I didn't mention this before because I wanted to save the news for this letter, but at the SPSEA Conference I won a scholarship for $1,650! It was something I applied for a while ago, and out of seventeen applicants, I was one of five winners. I was really hoping to get one, and I did! I also beat out an Albright student for next year's position of Eastern Region Secretary, which is a step above our local Kutztown chapter of SPSEA (Sam is President and Korey is Vice President). Being a region secretary plus Co-President and a Presidential Ambassador will look really great on my resume, as well as attending all of those conferences. I think I told you this before, but I also read a paper of mine at the annual spring Composition Conference, and it went over really well. I was given lots of praise by the professor who sat in on my presentation.

    I have more great news. I was also granted the Ruth Bonner Award, which is an English scholarship I received by having been nominated by one of my professors. I'll be getting a formal e-mail about it soon, so I'm not quite sure how much it's worth (it might be $500), but every little bit helps. I found out about this scholarship a week before your anniversary, and I was going to print out the e-mail and put it in your card. But the e-mail didn't come in time, and I figured it was no match against Todd and Mary's ultrasound anyway, haha. Plus, I wanted to see if I won the SPSEA scholarship so I could tell you about both of them at the same time in order to make you "doubly" proud of me.

4

*Think about all the other times you've been proud of me:
when I always came home with good grades because of working so
hard; when you watched me do well in countless softball games,
always there to cheer me on even if I was having an off night;
when you spent every Saturday morning watching me bowl at Bar
Don, even if I sometimes had a bad temper when I wasn't doing
well; when you saw me scurrying around the band field tooting my
flute during football games and competitions; and when you
caught a glimpse of me running across the stage to move props
during school musicals. Think of the times when you were proud
that I was a good friend, a caring friend, who never wanted to let
go of such special relationships, only to realize that sometimes
things just change and people move on. Think of the times when
we went out to dinner (which was a lot, haha!) and laughed
together, or when we lay in the living room watching a movie for
"video night," all the while enjoying each other's company. Think
about how far I've come—from being scared to death to go to
college to successfully completing almost three years now! Where
has the time gone?! I'm so glad I've made you proud parents.*

*With that said, it makes me sick to my stomach and utterly
upset to know that your pride in me and perception of me could
completely change all because of one thing. This one thing has
been taking over my mind all school year now, and it's something I
need to share with you even though I know it may change our
entire relationship. Since I don't know how to say this, I'll just be
blunt. I am interested in girls. It wasn't until this year that I
decided to acknowledge the feelings or attractions I've had for
certain females as something potentially beyond friendship. It has
been such a struggle to figure out if the connections I have to some
girls are simply emotional (since girls naturally share an
emotional connection), or if they're more than that. I've confided
in several people whom I knew would be open-minded about my*

situation and who might be of any help. But it wasn't they who "led me down this path," so to speak. It was my curiosity and need for answers that led me to seek a person or an experience that could help me confirm or nullify my attraction to the same sex. I went on a few dates, both with guys and girls. To cut out the stories in between, I'll just tell you that I started seeing a particular girl regularly, and I got the confirmation I needed to determine that I do indeed like girls and want to be in relationships with them. Because this girl realized she didn't want a relationship though, she and I have no longer been getting together. I was crushed, but I couldn't tell you about it. I've had to deal with the heartache on top of so much schoolwork, and it seems nearly impossible to get through the rest of the semester, especially now that I don't have plans with her to look forward to. She was the reason I was going to write this letter, and I was very hesitant to do so after things ended, but just because things didn't work out with her doesn't mean I'm going to refrain from dating girls. I just don't want to hide the truth anymore.

Right now you are undoubtedly crying or screaming or you're just too shocked to have a reaction. That's why I'm mailing this letter as opposed to talking to you in person. I wouldn't have been able to bear the looks on your faces when I told you. And I wanted you to have time to take this in and digest it on your own without me being there. I know that since the day I was born, you've probably imagined my wedding day or thought about the grandchildren I would give to you. You've had these expectations of who I am and who I will be, and I know this wasn't in your plan. It wasn't in mine either. But it's not something that will just go away. It's reality. I'm not saying I will never date a guy, fall in love, get married, and have children. I'm not closing myself off to the idea of guys. But even if I do end up with a girl, please don't be ignorant to the fact that same-sex couples can and do have

6

loving families just like other people. I honestly don't know what the future holds for me, so in sending you this letter, I'm just making you aware and preparing you for what's happening right now, whether you agree with it or not, whether you accept it or not. You've always said you will love me no matter what. I just hope you really meant it. I hope, in time, you will realize that I'm still the same Brianna who's always been your little girl. I love you!

Love,
Bri

The Reaction

Two days later, I was sitting next to Paul in Linguistics class. It was the day my parents would receive the letter. I wasn't just nervous; I was terrified. My cell phone was on my desk, and when it lit up with the dreaded words "House calling," I froze. Paul looked at me and grabbed my hand. I let my phone ring; after all, I was in class, and it wasn't ending for another half hour. "I'm in class now," I texted my mom. "I don't care, call us!" was her response. My heart was pounding, but I didn't leave class and call my parents. I sat there for thirty whole minutes, focused on nothing but the impending doom. I immediately regretted sending the letter. Now I couldn't hide. My parents knew, and there was no turning back.

When class ended, Paul walked outside with me, and we stood on the grass behind the library in a somewhat private location. I dialed the phone number, my stomach in knots. My mom answered, and so much was a blur after that. I *do* remember she sounded calm even in her extreme upset and fury. She said that she and my dad (and the whole family for that matter) would never accept it; I would ruin my life; I would destroy the family; Kutztown did this to me; Dad wanted to pull me out of school for that reason, and also because I'd have no future anyway, so why bother finishing college. I remember hearing a high-pitched sob in the background shrieking, "Who brainwashed you?! What's her name?!" It was my father. It sounded nothing like him. Hearing his cry made me even more sick to my stomach.

One thing my mom made sure to stress was that she and my dad still loved me, which was precisely why they were taking the news so hard. I wasn't sure I believed her. If they still loved me, why were they saying such horrible things? Why were they hurting me so much?

Paul called a mutual friend and asked her to pick us up at the library so we wouldn't have to walk. I was still on the phone, tears rolling down my cheeks, when I climbed into Cara's car and headed back to the apartment complex. My mom was still talking when we got there, so I stayed outside until our conversation ended, still very much unresolved. The last words my mom spoke were "Take care." We both hung up. I was numb. I had expected some shock, confusion, and lack of understanding; I knew they'd be upset. But I did *not* expect what had just happened. I cried the rest of the night, first in the comfort of Paul's apartment with several close friends trying their best to console my aching heart; and then alone, in the darkness and silence of my single bedroom.

*   *   *

There was a month until summer break, and it was hard to focus on end-of-semester papers and final exams. My mind was on my parents whom I'd yet to hear from a week after the phone call. I vaguely remember texting my mom to see how she was doing, but I didn't get a response. When Secretary's Day rolled around a few days later, I decided to call my mom as I did every year. I used a different phone for fear she would see my number and not answer.

"Hey, Mom."

"Hi," she managed in a depressed voice.

"Happy Secretary's Day."

"Thanks."

Silence.

"Okay, well I guess you don't wanna talk to me," I sighed.

"I can't," she said, trailing off and hanging up the phone.

I was defeated and didn't know what to do. I had the best relationship with my parents for twenty-one years, and now it was destroyed. All because of me. It's one thing to be punished for something you do. But I didn't *do* anything. I simply told the truth about who I am.

I soon sent an e-mail to my brothers that exposed my letter to Mom and Dad and confessed their hostile reaction. Todd sent a sympathetic response, assuring me they just needed time and offering his support whenever I needed it. My sister-in-law Katie sent a text from her and Matt that apologized and offered a place to stay if it came to that extreme. I was so thankful to have their love and understanding at a time I needed it most.

*   *   *

I received an e-mail a few days after the failed Secretary's Day call. My mom and dad wanted me to come home that weekend to talk. Although I was extremely intimidated, I went.

I can't begin to describe how I felt during that forty-five-minute car ride. In my mind, I was driving toward my death; not my literal death, but definitely that of my spirit and self-esteem. My mom wasn't home when I got there, so I sat in the basement and occupied myself on the computer in the meantime. I figured watching TV with my dad would be too uncomfortable for my already tense nerves. When the dogs started barking to signal my mom's arrival, I very reluctantly walked upstairs to face the music, afraid of how it would sound. I sat on the couch across from my parents. I was instructed to say nothing until I read the letter my mom handed me. There I sat, two against one; and as I read the words, cringing and crying as I made sense of their hurtful meaning, I was in utter disbelief that those words were written by a mother to her daughter.

*Note: This letter was typed exactly as written by my mom.

Bri—

As you read this, you'll probably cry, feel upset, even angry at times, hurt, and a million other feelings, something like I've been going through ever since I got your letter last week.
I didn't write sooner b/c I wanted to wait til I gave myself time to really think things through, unfortunately it also gave me a lot of time to hate you, be angry, feel sorry for you, feel sorry for myself, love you, and I'm at the point where I can't think anymore.

I just want to say again that I love you, and I know this is hard for you, as well as us. This is and will probably be the worst time of our lives as parents. I wake up every day praying it was a dream, not knowing if I can get out of bed and get through another day of work or idle chit chat with friends. I don't know if our lives will ever be the same again, if I'll ever be able to sleep or eat again, be happy, feel normal, yes it's that bad. The excitement of becoming a grandparent is gone, and I'm <u>very angry</u> at you for that. The thought of you graduating from college means nothing now. Kutztown is just a bad word to us. Nothing is the same. I keep telling myself it will get better, but I keep wishing it was last month at this time when my life was happy and sane. I can honestly say I've never seen your dad like this. I don't know that your relationship with him will ever be the same (I'm not saying this to *hurt you; I'm just being honest). You were honest with us and now it is my turn. This is the time of Dad's and my life where we should be happy, sitting back reflecting on the great job we've done—two kids married, grandkid on the way, and a daughter with only one year left of college. The next 20 years or so that we have left were supposed to be a reflection of all the hard work we put in over the last 31 years of marriage, and damn it Bri you have destroyed that! You really have no idea how this changes our lives forever.*

Dad and I have talked, and we thought we gave you the best of everything, in fact, more than your brothers ever got. We tried to show you what a loving family was like. We taught you values, morals, and to do the right thing. We taught you family traditions, which we thought meant a lot to you. We raised you well, so we thought. Yet this is a huge slap in the face. You are taking everything we spent 21 years teaching you and are basically saying "SCREW YOU MOM AND DAD, I DON'T' WANT TO BE LIKE YOU. I DON'T PLAN TO MARRY, HAVE KIDS, OR DO THE WHOLE FAMILY THING!" And what about me—imagine finding out the daughter who everyone says looks like you wants to be NOTHING LIKE YOU!!!!!!!

So then I have to ask myself why—WHY we ever bothered going to every softball game, bowling tournament, football games, band concerts, plays, and the million other little things we gave up ALL of our time for, b/c whether we would have gone to all those functions or said "The Hell With It," this would have happened. Obviously, we didn't need to be good parents—didn't need to support everything you did, didn't need to be on call 24/7, didn't need to set examples. It's like it didn't matter that we worked hard on our marriage so you weren't raised in a broken home like hundreds of other kids.

Basically Bri, life is all about choices. I chose not to run around and have affairs and put my kids through humiliation and turmoil. I chose not to be a whore who didn't care whether her kids had fathers or not. If you think Dad and I didn't have choices to go wrong over the years, you're wrong. It's hard being parents. Every choice we made, first and foremost, was what was best for you guys, ourselves always second. I had a choice—whether or not to have a third child or not!! Aren't you glad I made the "RIGHT" choice? That why I'm saying all of this—b/c I'm hoping you make the right choice in life. I hope you see that you deserve to give yourself time to find a nice guy and have a family. There is nothing more amazing in life!! Family means everything.

Do you have any idea everything you're giving up?

-Respect of family/friends
-The look in your brothers' and sister-in-laws' eyes when you tell them
-Walking down the aisle with your dad with tears in his eyes as he gives away his baby
-Your brothers seeing you get married, dancing with you at your wedding (how can this not bother you; you remember how it felt seeing your brothers get married. You're not giving them the opportunity to see you get married)
-Children (to a normal family)
-Respect from students when you teach
-What little Brandon will think of you in about a year or two when he realizes what it all means
-What your future nieces and nephews will think of their Aunt Bri Bri

-Todd or Matt will now never ask you to be godmother to their children (godmothers are people who are supposed to set good examples)
-What high school friends will think of you when they see you at the mall, at bonfires, work, or anywhere
-And so, so much more

I guess I just can't help wonder what happened to all the love poems you loved writing (you were such a romantic). What about sitting with a guy watching the sun set? What about when you said it's important for whoever you date that they get along well with your brothers? What about wanting to be like Miss Boyer? And Dad, I know he looked forward to the day he sat with his son-in-law at the kitchen table and had a few beers together. It's not just everything you're giving up, it's everything we're losing too.

How will you and I ever watch a DVD or love story together again? How will we ever go to the movies together—you know all the innuendos in the movies. How will I ever go to Kohl's with you to buy cute clothes so you'll look pretty for the guys? How will I ever buy you cutesy bras? How will Christmas ever be the same? What will we ever find to talk about now? How will we share those goofy moments again, take the dogs for a walk, sit on the deck. I know you say you're the same Brianna—but you know that's not really true—that's just what <u>you</u> want to believe. You say there are all kinds of families—have you tried to picture yourself going to the scary middle school for the first time, or Shawnee or even the high school. I remember how scared you were. Imagine a child who doesn't have the love and support you did to get through all the scary firsts. Imagine a child who goes to the middle school for the first time, scared and insecure, and then on top of that has to be humiliated b/c they have two moms or two

*dads—kids are cruel. Don't tell me there are all kinds of families
b/c you have no idea—you had a normal family and life. You're
just trying to convince yourself of that.*

*I feel Bri that you've never given yourself a chance to fall in love.
It's amazing and you need to at least experience it once in your life
before you decide it's not for you. I'm so afraid you'll do
something now that you'll regret later in life and won't forgive
yourself for. Have Dad and I ever steered you wrong—NEVER.
Once a long time ago, we had to have a big heart-to-heart with
Todd over a girl we truly felt was wrong for him. We gave him
ultimatums b/c we knew he could ruin his life if he didn't listen to
us—thankfully he listened to us, made the right choice, thanked us
later and was so much better off for it. He was young and need
our guidance. We would never guide any of you the wrong way.
We just ask that you listen and listen hard to everything we say and
know that we're doing what's best for you. I know you know we
want the best for you, it's just getting YOU to do what best for you
that's hard.*

*Also, we want nothing on Facebook or anywhere else. That means
doing what we say for now. Our world had been turned upside
down right now, but I WILL NOT let you turn other people's
worlds upside down as well, especially family, especially Mary and
Todd when they are so happy right now, no one. We've given you
way more than we've <u>ever</u> asked for in return. I've worked my ass
off for 31 years building this family and I thought I did a good job
until now. You will destroy it. You think your brothers will
understand—I doubt it. You think so many people will
understand—I doubt it. Who loves you more than Dad and I—NO
ONE, and look at the hard time we're having.*

15

*Lastly, you owe us! You owe us time to try to get through to you. You owe us finishing up college first and while doing so, keeping quiet right now. I don't want your grandparents to have heart attacks, which I seriously am afraid will happen, and how would you feel then? Mary doesn't need to hear bad news either with all her problems with the baby. If you want us to help you pay for and finish school and plan on continuing to live here, you will keep this to yourself, no matter what your friends think or say. Honestly, I don't care if that's a problem for you or not. These so called friends (and this is where you're going to get angry) mean nothing to me. I don't want to hear their names, or any stories about them right now. You say they are understanding and are okay with all this, but they're actually encouraging this and that's wrong. Right now you're at college in the little community where everything is fine and all your friends are cool with it b/c it's not a big deal to them, however, they aren't the ones who will be there for you when you fall apart after college. Next year after everyone graduates, when they're all off having families of their own, relocating to other places and off to find better jobs, they're not the ones who will be here for you—Dad and I will, as always. When you fall apart b/c people call you names, make fun of you, or hurt you, we'll still be here, but your friends will not. They're not here in the summer when you want to hang out, or at Christmas when you want to do things, so you must know when everyone is off and graduated, we'll be the ones here to help you pick up the pieces of your life—not them. And this is why we so much want you to rethink everything. The little community of college friends right now seems good to you—but face reality—**that won't last forever!** They're only around now b/c you're all in college together, but college won't last forever and real life is just around the corner. Again, who do you really believe cares more about you—them or us?*

*Bri, I've never told you how amazing I think you are. You are the one person I'm most proud of in the whole world, above my parents, husband, other kids, anyone I know. You always amazed me how hard you worked in school, got good grades while managing to play softball, do band, be a good friend and help others, and stayed on the right path and made the right choices in life. I still look at you and can't believe all you're doing in college—the clubs, working, being involved in activities, winning awards and scholarships, and still getting good grades. Wow, I think—that's my daughter! That's why when I send you those cards about how truly amazing you are, I mean them from the bottom of my heart!! You have such determination to do well for yourself and that's why I admire you and you make me more proud than anyone in my life ever has. That's what's so hard—you deserve to have a great life. You deserve to have respect from family and friends. You deserve to have a loving family. You would make a great daughter-in-law to some lucky parents b/c you make a great daughter. You deserve all this and so much more and instead you will be disrespected and called names and be made fun of, something you do not deserve. You are amazing. So I have to ask myself—**how can the person that makes me the most proud in life be the same person who put the biggest hole in my heart?***

It's all about choices ~~~

Hurt

Life didn't seem real in the moments of reading that letter. My teardrops stained each page. When I finally looked up at my parents, I didn't know what to say. I started the conversation by admitting I already came out to my brothers, and they were okay with it. My mom was angry I hadn't kept the disgraceful information to myself, but even more outraged they seemed to be accepting.

There was lots of crying, screaming, talking, and trying to counter each other's points. I had never seen my parents so severely disappointed in me, but I wasn't trying to hurt them. Liking women wasn't a random choice I decided to make. But in their twisted minds, it was as though I woke up one morning and thought, *I feel like ruining Mom and Dad's lives today. I think I'll start dating women and try to be* gay. Absolutely not! Looking back, there were so many signs growing up, and having crushes on women was something I had been experiencing for a long time. I didn't decide to be gay; I decided to own up to the feelings that weren't going to magically disappear.

It's hard to remember all the details of that "talk," but one comment my mom made stung particularly hard. I was trying to explain that my life would not be ruined by dating women. If I were an alcoholic, if I were addicted to drugs, if I were pregnant—all of *those* scenarios could potentially ruin my life. At that point, my mom said very matter-of-factly, "I would have rather had you tell me you were pregnant with a married black man's child." I was speechless.

*   *   *

I went back to Kutztown for the last two weeks of the semester. While there, I received another letter in the mail from my mom:

Hey Bri—

Listen, I don't mean to upset you, but I've been thinking about something and just wanted to share it with you. I really would like it if we just skipped Mother's Day this year. I can't bear to read a sentimental card from you right now. I know you love me so let's leave it at that. I just can't deal with a card and gift right now and I hope you understand why. I've only ever wanted to be a mom, a good mom, just like you've only ever wanted to be the best you can as a student. When you get a bad grade, you feel like you've let yourself down or should have tried harder. I feel like I let you down and should have tried harder. All along I kinda thought I was an A/B+ mom, definitely not an A+ or perfect in any way, but better than average. I don't feel that way right now, so let's just leave Mother's Day for a better time. I know you're gonna say it's nothing I did, but this is how I feel. The thought of you possibly never getting your own Mother's Day card, or waking up to your 2 year old bringing you breakfast in bed, burnt toast and all on Mother's Day, or getting a flower in a Dixie cup, or a tiny traced handprint, or a poem they wrote that makes no sense to anyone but

you, a handmade clay pot or a Christmas tree ornament, or go to
your own parent-teacher conference, I just can't get out of my
head right now. So please, no card, no gift. I don't need anything
anyway, and wanted to let you know before you bought something.

Love,
Mom

It absolutely broke my heart. Just because I admitted my interest in women, my mom assumed I would never live a normal life with a partner and children. A non-traditional family was too unorthodox for her to imagine. Essentially, my mom requested to skip the holiday because she couldn't bear to be acknowledged as my mother that year. Mother's Day involves the pride of being a mother, and she was no longer proud to have me as her daughter—her *gay* daughter.

Summer from Hell

I reluctantly went home for the summer after those final two weeks of school. When I first stepped into my bedroom, my jaw dropped. Everything deemed "girly" was gone: the pink canopy above my bed, old photos of female friends and me, ballerina wall decorations from when I was little, all the dresses from various dances I went to throughout high school, etc. The 2 x 4-foot collage my mom made for my high school graduation, which was covered in pictures of me from birth to age eighteen, was completely ripped apart and laid there for me to see. When I confronted my mom and asked why she did such a thing, she told me the girl in those pictures was her daughter, and she didn't know who *I* was. My hurt was mixed with a flare of anger. How dare she say that! Just because I discovered something about myself didn't mean I was any less her daughter. I was still the same Brianna she loved for twenty-one years!

*   *   *

The summer was filled was ups and downs, but the downs stuck more clearly in my memory. There was a certain Fourth of July blowout that resulted in a houseful of people screaming at each other all over me. It was my mom and dad against everyone else who didn't give a shit that I came out of the closet because *they* still loved me.

On any given evening when my mom and I watched TV and a gay character came into the mix, she'd change the channel or leave the room. Anything "gay" reminded her of me, and she didn't want to think about it. One time, she claimed homosexuality was becoming some type of fad. "Why is everyone gay all of a sudden?" she asked, "And why is it all over television?!"

At random, my mom would sit me down on one of her "bad days" and ask the same questions she had asked time and time again, the answers to which she refused to believe or accept. In her multiple attempts to have me look at the situation from her point of view, she always ended up making such hurtful, offensive statements. Since my words were clearly not getting through to her, I often just sat and cried, staring blankly at a piece of furniture in the room while half-listening to her negative spews.

During one such conversation, my mom admitted something very serious. When she was only a few weeks pregnant with me, her mom was rushed to the hospital. When my mom heard the news, she blurted this without even thinking: "Please, God, don't take my mother. Take my baby. I don't even know it yet." She instantly regretted those words and thought, as punishment, she would miscarry. She didn't. My mom thought I'd be born with some type of deformity. I wasn't. My mom thought something would happen to me as a child. It didn't. Until I was thirteen years old, my mom was convinced she'd somehow be punished for that awful prayer, but she never was. I was a happy, healthy baby who lived a normal, trauma-free life.

As I sat and listened to this story with tear-filled eyes, I started to feel sorry for my mom and her chronic paranoia. My sympathy instantly went away, though, when her story ended with,

"I just didn't think God would wait *twenty-one years* to punish me." What a knife to my heart. In her eyes, my homosexuality wasn't a pre-determined lifestyle; it was her punishment for a comment she made twenty-one years ago. If she had never made that wish upon her unborn child, that child (me) would be "normal."

She just didn't get it, and I was afraid she never would.

*   *   *

After much heartache and tears that season, the fall semester finally arrived, and I went back to Kutztown for my senior year. It was wonderful to be "home" again with my "family" since my actual home didn't feel like much of one anymore. Because I didn't have to tell my mom where I was going or with whom I was going, the tension between us had slightly dissipated. Whenever I *was* home, however, I adopted a new habit: lying.

Being honest did nothing but create awkwardness and hostility, so I started lying as an attempt to keep the peace. For a while, it was my only outlet. It allowed me to be happy with whomever I was dating, while simultaneously pleasing my mom because she thought I was single. "Single" equaled "straight" in her eyes. She even admitted it once. According to her, when I was single, she hoped I'd meet a great guy and realize it was all just a phase. Right.

The calm of the storm never lasted long, though. Something would inevitably happen to expose the truth, and turmoil would resume. One time I tried being honest about a new girl I was dating, but the result was no better, so back to lying I went.

*   *   *

A year and a half after coming out, I was still keeping all girls a secret from my parents, and it killed me inside. I tried

23

reaching out to my mom. From cover to cover I read *Love, Ellen: A Mother/Daughter Journey*, the personal account of Betty DeGeneres coming to terms with her own daughter's sexual orientation. I gleaned such a combination of knowledge, comfort, and understanding from her book. I knew if my mom read it, she'd be able to understand me a little better. Again, I was wrong. Handing her the book turned into another hurtful talk. "I don't care about Ellen and her mom. Nothing in that book can change my mind," she claimed.

Upon promising I'd still get married and have children (always a dream for her only daughter), I was completely shut down: "If you *ever* decide to get married to a woman, I will *not* be there!" Before walking to my room, defeated once again, my mom reluctantly took the book and agreed to read it if she had the time. Ever since, it has been collecting dust on the same shelf she placed it on that night. I guess watching reality TV every night is more important than salvaging our relationship.

Updates

Now, in January 2012, as long as the subject of my homosexuality isn't mentioned, my mom and I get along okay. We maintain a semblance of "loving mother and daughter" that fools everyone into believing all is well at the Pritchard household. Only it isn't. The hidden tension has caused me to resent my parents, my mother specifically. My dad and I don't talk about it; he hears everything through my mom. I respect him more for "butting out" and not wanting to know.

An update on my brothers . . . After they got caught covering for me and were hollered at by Mom for suggesting we seek counseling, I'm more cautious about opening up to them about my love life. Now that my brothers have children of their own, they not only have *their* relationship with my parents to worry about, but also their *children's* relationship to Grammy and Pop Pop, and I don't want to interfere with that.

The only family members I don't have to hide my life from are my aunt, uncle, and cousins on my mom's side of the family. Ever since that Fourth of July blowout at their house, they've welcomed me whenever I needed a listening ear—or a strong drink!

To this day, my Kutztown friends are my biggest support system. They've been there for me through all my tears, and after spending so much time together through the years, they know me better than anyone. A part of me has been missing ever since graduation, but I know that despite the physical distance between us, I can always count on their friendship.

*   *   *

Recall the section of my mom's letter that forbade me to come out to my grandparents:

> *"Lastly, you owe us! You owe us time to try to get through to you. You owe us finishing up college first and while doing so, keeping quiet right now. I don't want your grandparents to have heart attacks, which I seriously am afraid will happen, and how would you feel then?"*

To this day I haven't told them. Not because I didn't want to, but because I didn't want to deal with the wrath of my mother. Two months ago, one of my grandfathers passed away. When the minister encouraged us to write him goodbye letters, I knew what I needed to do. During our private viewing hour before the funeral, I placed my letter in Pop's casket, nestling it among the "I love you" and "I miss you" letters from other family members. It read:

11/25/11

Dear Pop,

It's Brianna, your only granddaughter. I hope you heard my speech at the funeral service. I really wanted to read it myself, but I knew I wouldn't be able to get through the words because I'd be crying so hard. Pop, I know I was always caught up in my busy life and didn't spend as much time with you as you would have *liked, but that doesn't mean I didn't love you. Whether it was a box of gum, candy, a $20 bill, or something as simple as a laugh or smile, I could always count on you to make my day. You were such a loving, generous man. People who barely knew you would comment on what a great guy you were. You had such a pleasant, outgoing personality that people noticed and appreciated. Your death still hasn't hit me. It almost feels like a bad dream I'm waiting to wake up from. In my mind, you can't really be gone.*

There's something I need to tell you. You don't know the whole me, Pop. It would break my heart every time you said, "You know, I'd like to see my granddaughter get married before I die." I wanted to tell you this so badly, but I was afraid of your reaction. Mom and Dad had such a hard time (and still do) accepting it, and Mom honestly thought you might have a heart attack and die if you found out, so I kept my mouth shut. I can't anymore, though. I need you to know that I'm gay. Dating girls doesn't feel wrong or different; it feels exactly right. I'm still the same Brianna you've always known, but I'm just not going to end up with a man. I still want to get married and raise a family; it just won't happen the way you expected it to. All you've ever wanted was for me to be happy, and I really, truly am. I can guarantee you that I will live a happy life with my future partner and children. Please find the understanding in your heart to accept me, and if you can, please give Mom the strength to come around and be a part of my entire life. I hate lying to her about my dating life, but right now I don't feel she's giving me any other choice. Until she stops hurting, I can't say anything that will hurt her even more. I love Mom so much, but I wish she would love me for exactly who I am, and not who she wants me to be.

Thanks for letting me get that off my chest. I pray you still love me. I know I'll always love you, and I'll miss you deeply. Goodbye, Pop.

Love always,
Brianna

27

Yes, I put a "coming out" letter in my grandfather's casket. I didn't tell anyone, especially not my mom. That letter was closure for me, my last chance to open up to Pop before I said goodbye. It was quite a bold move, but one I had to make.

Hope

After dating a particular girl for a while and sharing an undeniable connection, I decided to tell my mom about her. My intention wasn't to stir the pot and upset her for the millionth time. I somehow knew this relationship would last, so I figured it was time to rip off the Band-Aid and expose the truth. After listening to some basic information about Shelby, my mom said, "I'm just glad your grandfather is gone so he doesn't have to witness your lifestyle." I sat there, smoke coming out of my ears, wondering how she had the nerve to make such a callous statement. Instead of speaking out in defense, I silently walked upstairs to bed, my eyes burning with tears.

*   *   *

I don't know how many more hurtful comments I'll have to endure. I don't know if my parents will ever come around—if they'll ever accept me as their gay daughter. I *do* know, however, that I'm proud of who I am and who I'll become. I also know, without a doubt, that I am happy. After many failed relationships, I've finally found my dream girl.

Shelby and I complete each other, filling all the voids left by incompatible partners. She came into my life, swept me off my feet, and hasn't put me down ever since. Together, we've been floating on Cloud 9, and that's where we plan to stay. Every minute spent with her is magic. I don't know what sort of spell has been cast on us, but we're sure it's eternal. As far as luck goes, we've both hit the jackpot, and our lives are now richer than ever.

Lately, whenever I happen to glance at the clock at 11:11, I have a different wish in mind. As I smile and think of Shelby, I now wish for a certain four-letter word, and I know she'll make it come true.

Inspired Poems
by Brianna

"Breaking"

They

        and their chilling words

        pierce my soul like

        winter's sharpest icicles.

        To mask the pain, I

will

        remain an outer shell of strength,

        but secretly curl up inside myself

        at night, emotionally beaten and bruised,

never

        able to overcome the bigotry

        of my own flesh and blood.

        Mom and Dad: two people

        programmed to protect,

accept,

        and love unconditionally.

        But here I am, broken,

        Still breaking.

        Because I have distorted the

"me"

        who was once their

        perfect, innocent daughter.

        The price to pay for finding myself

        was losing them.

"Boiling Point"

Water rests inside a pot,
peaceful and undisturbed.
All is calm, until She speaks.
With each word uttered, the temperature rises,
creating a simmer of latent fury.
More words,
They sting, they burn.
The water's boil draws near,
losing control of its temper.
More claims,
A drop of food coloring diffuses,
forming angry red bubbles that climb
higher, higher…
More comments,
The water feverishly rises,
threatening to spill over the edge
and escape its boundaries.
New warnings,
The water seethes,
inching higher, higher…
At last, She reaches to turn down the burner,
but it's too late.
The water surges out of the pot,
scalding and staining everything it touches.
The mess is made, the damage done.
Everything's been tainted.

Author's Note

Dear readers,

My intention was to publish this memoir in January 2012, but I never did. I think I was waiting for more to happen with my parents; I knew my story wasn't finished. It's now November 2012, and there have been plenty more fights, harsh words, and tears since I first introduced the idea of Shelby to my mom. In a positive light, though, my parents and I have also shared some tender, loving moments in the past ten months, so I've chosen to focus on them rather than add more hurt to my story. I like that it ends with a feeling of hope, love, and vulnerability. Although I won't go into detail, I'll share three major updates with you:

1) I came out to all my grandparents, and none of them had heart attacks as my mom predicted.
2) My parents have come a long way with their acceptance of me. We haven't fought in months, and I'm very grateful for that.
3) My wish for love came true. Shelby and I recently celebrated our nine-month anniversary, and our relationship is still going strong.

Thanks again to everyone who has supported me these past few years. Without you, I might've crumbled mentally and emotionally. Instead, I've become a much stronger woman.

Feel free to contact me via e-mail with any comments or personal stories you'd like to share: bripritchard896@gmail.com.

Sincerely,
Brianna

January 2012

Me   Shelby